SONG CHARTING
MADE EASY
A Play-Along Guide to the Nashville Number System

T0084176

To access audio visit:
www.halleonard.com/mylibrary

Enter Code
6768-4641-4936-5279

This book is dedicated to my family, who believes in me;
my wife, Jaime, who stands by me;
and my daughter, Kendall, who continues to inspire me.

Special thanks to Rascal Flatts.

ISBN 978-1-4234-6367-2

HAL•LEONARD®
CORPORATION
7777 W. BLUEMOUND RD. P.O. BOX 13819 MILWAUKEE, WI 53213

In Australia Contact:
Hal Leonard Australia Pty. Ltd.
4 Lentara Court
Cheltenham, Victoria, 3192 Australia
Email: ausadmin@halleonard.com.au

Visit Hal Leonard Online at
www.halleonard.com

Preface

As a musician who has played countless dates with bands with little or no rehearsal, I always struggled to find a charting system that I could rely on. Having my degree in music, writing the song out in standard notation was an option, but as a drummer, looking at countless measures of time would tell me very little about what the rest of the band was doing. How would I know where I was if I got lost somewhere near measure 78? This made standard notation impractical. So I would always write these "chicken scratch" cheat sheets in my own shorthand that would mean nothing to anyone but me. The problem with this, of course, arose when I subbed the gig out; my cheat sheets were useless. I also watched on many occasions the rest of the band frantically rewriting their chart when the singer said that he wanted to do that song a step lower because his voice hurt. It wasn't until I moved to Nashville in 1997 that I was exposed to the Number System of writing charts. It was there that I found a system in place that all of the professional musicians understood. Rather than writing separate charts for each individual musician, the leader wrote one chart that the entire band could read: a highly detailed roadmap containing all of the chords and rhythms needed to produce a great performance. Since the system is based on intervals and not actual chord names, it was easy to change the key. This system was not, however, entirely foreign to me. I had studied a similar system in music theory classes in college.

The Number System has its origins in the Baroque period with figured bass, but is most closely related to Roman numeral analysis from the 1800s. It was in the 1950s that this system was adapted for use by studio musicians in Nashville who were looking for a way to accurately chart the songs of the day. Throughout its history, the system has always relied on the musician to use their musical creativity and interpret the chart rather than read a chart note for note.

I feel the reason why the Number System is not used by more people is simply because no one has presented the system in a methodical manner that the average musician can easily understand. This system has always been used by professional studio musicians and just "passed along" from player to player—like a secret code. People outside the business have never had it sufficiently explained to them. Most music teachers have never even heard of it because, at this point, the system is rarely taught in school. The truth is, the Number System is easy to learn, easy to write, and easy to read. What could take a dozen pages to chart in standard notation can easily be replaced with a single page of music. Let me give you an example: I looked through the Hal Leonard library and found a fully transcribed score of Aerosmith's "Livin' on the Edge." Each musician's sheet music was four pages long, and with music for guitar, bass, drums, and keyboard, that's sixteen pages of music. This lengthy score can be replaced with one chart written by hand in five minutes! What happens if you change the key? In standard notation every note on the page would be wrong: But with the number system you are still good to go.

The bottom line is this: If you want to dictate exactly what every musician is playing at every given moment, then use standard musical notation to write out separate charts. If, however, you want to hand every musician in the band a single, concise, and versatile chart that allows the use of his or her own creativity to fill in the blanks, then you will love this system.

Table of Contents

How to Use This Book

This book is designed for any rhythm section player to be able to study and learn the Number System on their own. Each chapter introduces new concepts and reinforces them with audio examples. You then have the unique opportunity to apply these new concepts playing along with some of the world's best session musicians featured on recordings minus your instrument. Not only will you learn to read number charts, you will also learn to write them. Each chapter contains dictation examples that you can transcribe using the Number System to reinforce what you have learned. After learning the concepts in this book, you will comfortably be able to read any number chart handed to you on a live gig or recording session. You will also possess a powerful shorthand for writing your own charts.

This book can also be used in a classroom setting or rhythm section class. The concepts can be taught to all instrumentalists simultaneously, and the songs can be performed as a group.

As you read along, you will frequently notice words printed in the *italics* font. To help you better understand the terminology used with the Number System, words and phrases printed in italics are clearly defined in the glossary section in the back of the book.

About the Songs

Each song was written to demonstrate the concepts that have been introduced by that point in the book. There are five versions of each song: the first is the full mix, the second is minus guitar, the third is minus keyboards, the fourth is minus bass, and the fifth is minus drums. While you will choose the appropriate version to play along with, I think you will find the other versions helpful if you want to know more about the parts the session musicians played. For example, the keyboard parts are very easy to pick out on the "minus guitar" track. Using the included charts, these songs can also be performed in a rhythm section class or, for that matter, with your own band. Six of the songs were recorded with a male lead vocal and four with a female. Provided for each song is the tempo, feel, and key that it was recorded in as well as a suggested key for the opposite gender to sing the song comfortably. Incidentally, all of the songs were written "gender neutral" for this very reason. The lyrics to the songs are included in the back of the book. I had originally planned on using session vocalists to sing the songs, but since I expected you to be able to sing them, I decided that my wife, Jaime, and I would do all of the vocals.

The Number System is by far the easiest and most versatile song charting system in the world. The charts are designed so that the same chart can be used by every member of the band and they can be written so quickly that a three minute song can be accurately charted in about five minutes! So forget what you have heard about the Number System before, and let's start fresh.

CHAPTER ONE:
Basic Principles of the Number System

The first thing you need to understand is what the numbers stand for. Each number refers to a *scale degree* of the *major scale*. Instead of using the familiar *DO–RE–MI–FA–SOL–LA–TI*, we will use 1–2–3–4–5–6–7. But why use numbers? Why not use the given name of each note? The simplest answer is that a C note is always a C. If you write a traditional *chart* in the *key* of C, and the singer wants to change it to the key of F, you are forced to write a new chart. However, if you are using numbers, and you want to play in the key of C, then C=1, D=2, and so on. Now if you want to change the key, it is as simple as reassigning F as your new 1. Now F=1, G=2, and so on. In other words, write the chart once, and it can be played in any key.

In the key of C, C–D–E–F–G–A–B equals 1–2–3–4–5–6–7. Instead of jumping around to all of these *chords* right from the start, let's just start with the most common ones: 1–4–5. There are literally thousands of *songs* that you can play using only these three chords. As a number is written down, there are certain things that can be assumed about that numeral:

- Any number standing alone represents a chord that should be played for one measure.

- All numbers represent *a major chord*, unless otherwise notated.

- The bass player should always play the *root* note, unless otherwise notated

In addition, you can also assume that the default *time signature* is *4/4*. In other words, unless otherwise specified, you'll be counting four *beats* per measure or *common time*.

So let's get started with our first chart.

1   4   1   5

This group of numbers tells us to play the 1 chord for one measure, the 4 chord for one measure, the 1 chord for one measure, and then the 5 chord for one measure. So in the key of C, the chords would be C–F–C–G.

Example A

1   4   1   5

As we add a second *phrase* of music, we write it below the first to clearly outline the phrasing. This is my favorite feature of this system!

Example B

1   4   1   5

4   1   5   5

 **DICTATION:**

Example One

It is very important to me that you not only learn to read these charts, but write them as well. Therefore, each chapter will include a musical example for you to listen to and write down. The answers are at the back of the book—no peeking! Let's see how you do with this one:

 TRACK 3

_ _ _ _ _ _   _ _ _ _ _ _   _ _ _ _ _ _   _ _ _ _ _ _

_ _ _ _ _ _   _ _ _ _ _ _   _ _ _ _ _ _

 **CHART TOOLS:**

Section Markers

As you take a look at our first chart, you'll notice that the chart is divided up into sections. The sections are labeled as follows:

- "I" for _intro_
- "V" for _verse_
- "Ch" for _chorus_
- "Solo" indicates an instrumental solo

Our first chart uses the 1, 4, and 5 chords. One thing I would like you to notice about this chart is how easy it is to identify not only the phrases, but the entire _form_ of the song at a glance. The intro is made up of two four-measure phrases, while both the verse and chorus contain four separate four-measure phrases, making each section sixteen measures long. This type of immediate recognition of the form is not possible with standard notation. Using this system, you can stop counting bars and start listening to the music around you.

 **CHORD SPOTLIGHT:**

Suspended 4th Chord

Although not listed on the chart, the guitar player's use of the sus4 chord is worth mentioning. You can hear it prominently in measures three and four of our first song. The sus4 is played by replacing the 3rd of our root–3rd–5th triad with a 4th. This suspension is usually resolved back to the major triad.

As you get ready to play down this first chart, remember that there are five versions of each song (full arrangement and tracks minus guitar, keyboards, bass, and drums). Now choose your version, and let's get ready to jam!

 TRACKS 4–8

Rock and Roll Will Set Me Free

Our first song is in the style of sixties British rock. We will only be using the three chords covered in this chapter. To the right of each new section, I have the pattern that the drummer will be playing written in parentheses. This can also be very helpful to non-drummers in the formation of your own parts. Remember that this system relies on musicians to use their own creativity and musical intuition to fill in the blanks. So listen to what everyone else is playing, try to fit in musically, and—most of all—have fun!

Recorded with a male vocal in the key of E. Suggested female key: A

ROCK AND ROLL WILL SET ME FREE

I)   *OPEN HI-HAT* (♩ ♩ ♫ ♩)

1	4	5	5
1	4	5	5

V)   *HI-HAT* (♩ ♩ ⅄ ♪ ♫)

4	4	1	1
4	4	1	1
5	5	4	4
1	1	5	5

CH)   *OPEN HI-HAT* (♩ ♩ ♫ ♩)

1	4	5	5
1	4	5	5
4	5	1	1
4	5	1	1

V)

4	4	1	1
4	4	1	1
5	5	4	4
1	1	5	5

CH)

1	4	5	5
1	4	5	5
4	5	1	1
4	5	1	1

SOLO)   *RIDE* (♫ ♩ ♫ ♩)

5	5	4	4
5	5	4	5

CH)

1	4	5	5
1	4	5	5
4	5	1	1
4	5	1	1
4	5		

HI-HAT (♩ ♩ ⅄ ♪ ♫)

1	1	1

CHAPTER TWO:
Minor Chords, Diamonds

As we learned in Chapter One, all chords are assumed to be major unless otherwise notated. If you want a particular chord to be a *minor chord*, simply place a dash to the right side of the number.

6-

This example in the key of D makes typical use of the 6- chord.

Example C

1	4	1	5
6-	4	1	5

When talking about the *Number System*, the "numbers" are only half of the story. In addition to the numbers, there is a multitude of symbols and shorthand to help us notate many of the rhythmical situations that we will encounter. One of the most common is the *diamond*.

Diamonds

The diamond bears a striking resemblance to the *whole note*, and for good reason. It's placed around a chord when you want the rhythm to stop and the chord to be held out for the entire measure.

1	4	6-	5	
◇1	◇4	◇6-	◇5	◇1

Example D

There are a few things to keep in mind about diamonds: Even though it tells you to play a whole note, the producer may tell one or more players to ignore the symbol and play through. This is very common. In addition, the drummer can use his discretion to set up the figures. Here is what it would sound like if the guitar player plays through and the drummer sets up the diamond figures.

Example E

DICTATION:

TRACK 12

This new dictation example will make use of our new concepts (the 6- chord and diamond), so listen carefully.

Example Two

— — — — — —   — — — — — —   — — — — — —   — — — — — —

— — — — — —   — — — — — —   — — — — — —   — — — — — —   — — — — — —

CHART TOOLS:

Bridge, Outro, and Fermata

In our next chart you will notice some new section markers:

- "Br" for *bridge*
- "Out" for *outro*

Also, at the end of the outro you will see the following symbol 𝄐. This is a *fermata*, or what is sometimes referred to as a "bird's eye." It extends the value of the note indefinitely until the band is cued to stop. Once you hear it, you will get the idea.

TRACKS 13–17

The Rest of Me

Our next chart is an up-tempo rock song, so keep the energy high! Watch out for all of the new stuff we learned in this chapter.

Recorded with a male vocal in the key of E. Suggested female key: B♭.

THE REST OF ME

I) (CRASH ♪ ♩ ♫ ♩ | ♩ ♫. ♫ ♩)
1   5   4   5
1   5   4   4

V) (HI-HAT ♪ ♩ ♫ ♩)
1   1   5   5
4   4   5   5
1   1   5   5
6-   5   4   4   ◇4

CH) (OPEN HI-HAT ♪ ♩ ♫ ♩)
1   5   4   5
6-   4   5   5
1   5   4   5
6-   4   5   ◇5

I)
1   5   4   5
1   5   4   4

V)
1   1   5   5
4   4   5   5
1   1   5   5
6-   5   4   4   4

CH)
1   5   4   5
6-   4   5   5
1   5   4   5
6-   4   5   5

BR) (RIDE ♪ ♩ ♫ ♩)
6-   6-   4   4
1   1
5   5   5   5

CH)
◇1   ◇5   ◇4   ◇5
◇6- ◇4   (CRAZY FILL) 5   5
1   5   4   5
6-   4   5   5

OUT) (CRASH ♪ ♩ ♫ ♩)
1   5   4   5
1   5   4   5
1   5   4   5
1   5   4   5   ◇1

CHAPTER THREE:

2- Chords, Split Bars

 **NEW CHORD:**

 TRACK 18

2-

Here is a musical example in the key of E using the 2- chord:

Example F

```
1      2-      4      5
                              ⌢
                             ⌢•
6-      4      1      5     ◇1◇
```

So far, all of the music examples have contained one chord per measure. But what if you want to notate more than one chord per measure?

 **NEW CONCEPT:**

Split Bars

The *split bar* is the shorthand used when you want to play two chords in one measure. It is notated as follows: **1   4**

In the above situation, the 1 chord would be played for beats one and two, and the 4 chord would be played for beats three and four.

Here is a musical example using a split bar:

 TRACK 19

Example G

```
6-        5        4        2-
                          ⌢•
4   1    6-  5    ◇1◇
```

The split bar notation can also be used to indicate four chords per measure. In this situation, you would change chords every beat.

 TRACK 20

Example H

```
                                    ⌢•
1        2-        1  4  6-  5    ◇1◇
```

Note to drummers: You may be thinking, "What difference does it make to me where the chord changes are in the measure?" Well, the answer is: a lot! You may be entrenched in a syncopated groove, but when the chord changes start happening in the middle of the measure, you and all of the other rhythm section players need to adjust.

Example I

$$\begin{array}{cccc} 4 & 1 & 4 & \overset{\frown}{5} \\ \end{array}$$

$$\begin{array}{cccccc} \underline{6\text{-} \quad 4} & \underline{2\text{-} \quad 5} & 1 & \langle 1 \rangle \end{array}$$

 **DICTATION:**

Example Three

In this dictation example, pay close attention to the rhythm of the changes. Ask yourself, "Are the chords changing every four beats or every two?" When you're working this out, feel free to rewind the example and count it out. It is better to listen back a few more times and get it right than to rush through.

‑ ‑ ‑ ‑ ‑ ‑ ‑ ‑ ‑ ‑ ‑ ‑ ‑ ‑ ‑ ‑ ‑ ‑ ‑ ‑ ‑ ‑ ‑ ‑ ‑ ‑ ‑ ‑

‑ ‑ ‑ ‑ ‑ ‑ ‑ ‑ ‑ ‑ ‑ ‑ ‑ ‑ ‑ ‑ ‑ ‑ ‑ ‑ ‑ ‑ ‑ ‑ ‑ ‑ ‑ ‑ ‑ ‑ ‑ ‑ ‑ ‑ ‑

CHART TOOLS:

Channel and Turnaround

This song makes very good use of a unique song section called the *channel*, or *pre-chorus*. The channel is the last section of the verse leading into the chorus. It usually contains a different chord progression than the rest of the verse and can vary in length depending on the song. Not all songs have a channel, and it is not always marked, but it is very important to be able to identify it in a rehearsal situation as it can be a frequent starting point when running the chorus. In the next song, the channel is the third line of the verse.

Also introduced is the new section marker *turn*. "Turn" is short for *turnaround*, which usually employs the same phrase as the intro, only it's not at the beginning of the song.

- "Cha" for *channel*
- "Turn" for *turn*

Shooting Stars

This track is what I would describe as a bohemian pop song. The feel is a half-time shuffle, so pay close attention to this new groove.

Recorded with a male vocal in the key of G. Suggested female key: B♭.

SHOOTING STARS

I) 6- 1 4 2- 6- 1 4 2- (HI-HAT ♫ ♩ ♫ ♩)

V) 6- 1 4 2- 6- 1 4 2- (HI-HAT ♫ ♩ ♫ ♩)
6- 1 4 2- 6- 1 4 5

CHA) 2- 4 5 2- 4 5 (HI-HAT ♩ ♩ ♫ ♩)

CH) 1 5 2- 4 5 (RIDE ♫ ♩ ♫ ♩)
1 5 2- ◇4◇

TURN) 6- 1 4 2- 6- 1 4 2-

V) 6- 1 4 2- 6 1 4 2-
6- 1 4 2- 6 1 4 5

CHA) 2- 4 5 2- 4 5

CH) 1 5 2- 4 5
1 5 2- 4 5
1 1

BR) 2- 4 5 2- 4 5 (OPEN HI-HAT ♩ ♩ ♫ ♩)
6- 4 2- 4 5

SOLO) 1 5 2- 4 5 (RIDE ♫ ♩ ♫ ♩)

CH) 1 5 ◇2-◇ 4 5
1 5 2- 4 5

CH) 1 5 2- 4 5
1. 5 2- 4 5 ◇1◇

CHAPTER FOUR:
Accidentals, Uneven Split Bars

 **NEW CONCEPT:**

Sharps and Flats

Sharps and *flats* (collectively know as *accidentals*) are borrowed from standard notation and are used to raise or lower chords. For example, in the key of G, the note A is the 2nd scale degree, but if you wanted to lower it by a half step, then you would write A♭, or ♭2 in the Number System. To illustrate the difference, here is a short passage using both 2 and ♭2 chords.

TRACK 28

Example J

$$1 \qquad 2 \qquad 1 \qquad ♭2 \qquad \boxed{1}$$

This opens up a whole world of new chords, my favorite of which is next.

 **NEW CHORD:**

♭7

The ♭7 is a common, yet powerful chord. The root of this chord is a whole step down from the 1 chord. So if you are in the key of G, the ♭7 would be a F chord. Here is a short musical passage to illustrate the powerful sound of this chord.

TRACK 29

Example K

1	5	4	5
1	5	4	4
♭7	4	1	1
♭7	4	⌢⟨1⟩	

Songwriters frequently use it to introduce the bridge because of its unique sound, but you'll find that it can be used almost anywhere within the framework of a song.

Uneven Split Bars

In the last chapter, you learned how to play split bars. These work great when you want to change chords on beat one and beat three, but what if you want the second chord to happen on beat four instead? *Uneven split bars* take care of this scenario perfectly.

Uneven split bars use dots above the numbers to show you how long to hold each chord. One dot equals one beat. In 4/4 time, you could have your first chord last three beats with the next chord on beat four. In the key of G, this would be notated as follows:

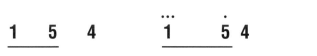

Listen to the clear difference between an evenly split bar and an unevenly split one.

Example L

This system can also be applied to 4/4 measures with three chords. In this next example, you would play the 4 chord on beat one for two beats, switch to the 1 chord on beat three, and then the 5 chord on beat four.

This next example will show you some of the many rhythmic variations you can notate with this "dot" system.

Example M

Author's Note: There is a common practice to use a dot over a number to denote a short note. I would suggest not using the dot for this purpose since it is already used for uneven split bars and could easily cause confusion. We'll be using a *marcato* for a short note (see Chapter Five). You should be aware in reading other people's charts that the dot is occasionally used in this way.

Example Four

This dictation example contains some tricky rhythms, so listen carefully.

TRACK 32

_ _ _ _ _ _ _   _ _ _ _ _ _ _   _ _ _ _ _ _ _   _ _ _ _ _ _ _   _ _ _ _ _ _ _

Dynamics

Dynamics are the markings that tell us how loud or soft to play. The most common are *piano* (***p***) which is Italian for "soft," and *forte* (***f***) which is Italian for "loud." Typically you won't see a lot of dynamic markings on number charts, but that doesn't mean you can't use them. A common term seen on a chart is *breakdown*, which usually implies that the section (usually the chorus) will be played at a lower dynamic level and with only sparse rhythm. It is commonly followed by a *crescendo* (⟨) which is written under the numbers where you want to get louder. You may also encounter a *decrescendo* which means to get softer.

Major 7th Chord

A *major 7th* chord is formed when you play a major 7th (counting up from the root of the chord) on top of a major triad. A Dmaj7 chord is voiced D–F♯–A–C♯. If you listen back to measure twelve of example K, you can hear the guitar player sneak in a major 7th chord.

TRACKS 33-37

Right Here

This song is a mid-tempo rock ballad. Watch for the dynamic markings that lead into the third chorus. Drummers should take notice that the verse pattern "rides" on the floor tom rather than the hi-hat.

Recorded with a male vocal in the key of A. Suggested female key: C.

RIGHT HERE

I)

1 4 6- 4 (CRASH ♩ ♩ ♫ ♩)

1 4 6- ◇4◇

V)

1 4 6- 4 (R.H. ON FLOOR TOM. ♩ ♩ ♫ ♩)

1 4 6- 4

1 4 6- 4

5 4 5 ◇4MAJ7◇

CH)

1 5 ♭7 4̈ 5́ (RIDE ♩ ♩ ♫ ♩)

1 5 ♭7 4

2- 4 2- 4

TURN)

1 4 6- 4 (CRASH ♩ ♩ ♫ ♩)

V)

1 4 6- 4

1 4 6- 4

1 4 6- 4

5 4 5 4

CH)

1 5 ♭7 4̈ 5́

1 5 ♭7 4

2- 4 2- 4

BR)

♭7 4 1 1̈ 2́- (CRASH ♩ ♩ ♫ ♩)

♭7 4 2- 4 4

SOLO)

1 5 ♭7 4 (RIDE ♩ ♩ ♫ ♩)

1 5 ♭7 4

CHA)

2- 4 2- 4 ◢◣ 4

CH) BREAKDOWN

◇1◇ ◇5◇ ◇♭7◇ 4̈ 5́ ◥◤

1 5 ♭7 4

2- 4 2- 4

OUT)

1 5 ♭7 4 (RIDE ♩ ♩ ♫ ♩)

1 5 ♭7 4̈ 5́

1 5 ♭7 4

1 5 ♭7 4̈ 5́ ◇1◇

NEW CHORD:

 TRACK 38

3-

The 3- is a common chord, but it can be hard to identify if you are not used to hearing it. Here is the 3- in musical context played in the key of F.

Example N

1	3-	6-	4	
1	3-	4	5	1

In the first line, the 3- is used as a setup for the 6- chord, while in the second line, it's used as a passing chord on the way up to the 5.

This 3- is the last simple chord that will be introduced individually. 1, 2-, 3-, 4, 5, 6-, and $\flat$7 are some of the most common chords, and they've been used to ease you into hearing how and where the chords move. Remember, you can raise or lower almost any chord by a half step using flat and sharp symbols, so don't be surprised to see a $\sharp$4 or a $\flat$6, because they will pop up. The same goes for the *chord quality*. Any of the chords can appear as major or minor, so a 5- could be a possibility as well.

 NEW CONCEPT:

Marcato

The marcato, or "rooftop," is a symbol borrowed from big band charts. When placed over a chord, the symbol tells the musician to play that chord short.

Here is a musical passage using the marcato. The piano will play through the stop to keep the groove going.

TRACK 39

Example O

5	6-	4	5	
^1	^5	^4	^5	1

Here is the same musical example using diamonds in place of the marcatos. The impact on the music is quite different. As with the diamond, some players may be asked to play through the marcato signs for the desired musical effect.

Example P

Sometimes in the course of using a marcato, you may find a need to notate a measure in which no music is played. In this case, you can use an "X" to fill the space of a blank measure. For example, this figure:

would be played:

The marcato can also be used in a split bar. In this case, the first chord of the measure would be played for two beats, while the chord on beat three would be played short.

Example Q

1 5 4 5̂ 1 ◇ 1

While we are at it, the diamond can be used in the exact same fashion.

Example R

1 5 4 ⟨5⟩ 1 ◇ 1

Note to drummers: Remember, when the band is playing the short note, it is your responsibility to keep the band tight by setting up the figures.

DICTATION:

TRACK 43

Example Five

The 3- chord can be a hard one to hear at first, so be patient and use a tonal reference like a keyboard or guitar to help you pick it out. The marcato on the other hand is hard to miss!

_ _ _ _ _ _ _   _ _ _ _ _ _ _   _ _ _ _ _ _ _   _ _ _ _ _ _ _

_ _ _ _ _ _ _   _ _ _ _ _ _ _   _ _ _ _ _ _ _   _ _ _ _ _ _ _   _ _ _ _ _ _ _

CHART TOOLS:

Repeat Signs

This next tune makes use of a very common piece of musical shorthand—*repeat signs* (   ). These are used around sections that you want repeated. As you read down the chart, you will first see this symbol   . Make note of its location, because you will need it. As you read further, you will come across this symbol   . This one tells you to go back to where you saw the first one and play the entire section over. When you get to the second symbol on the repeat, you play past it to the next section. This is very handy notation in popular music!

TRACK 44-48

Reach Out

This is a fun, laid back, reggae song. It features the 3- chord as well as the marcato sign. Take note of the uneven split bar at the end of the solo. Notice how much shorter our chart is when we use the repeat sign—pretty cool!

Recorded with a female vocal in the key of D. Suggested male key: D.

KEY OF D

REGGAE ♩ = 82

REACH OUT

I)

‖: 1   3–   6–   4 5

SIDE STICK
1x (𝄾 ♩ x· x ♩ xx)

SNARE
2x (♩ ♩ ♩ ♩)

V)

1   3–   6–   4 5

SIDE STICK
1x (𝄾 ♩ x· x ♩ xx)

1   3–   6–   4 5

SIDE STICK
2x (♩ x· x ♩ ♩)

CH)

4 5 1 6– 4 5 1

4 5 1 6– 4   5 5̂ :‖

SIDE STICK
1x (𝄾 ♩ x· x ♩ xx)

SNARE
2x (♩ ♩ ♩ ♩)

SOLO)

1   3–   6–   4 5

1   3–   6–   4̈ 5́ 3–

RIDE
(♩ ♩ ♩ ♩)

BR)

2– 4 3– 6– 4 5 1

2– 4 3– 6– 4   5̂

HI-HAT
(♩ ♩ ♩ ♩)

CH)

4 5 1 6– 4 5 1

4 5 1 6– 4   5

4   5 5̂

SNARE
(♩ ♩ ♩ ♩)

OUT)

1   3–   6–   4 5

1   3–   6–   4 5

RIDE
(♩ ♩ ♩ ♩)

𝄐
⟨1⟩

21

CHAPTER SIX:
Chord Inversions, Pushes

 **NEW CONCEPT:** Chord Inversions

Up to this point, all of the chords we played have been in *root position*. What that simply means is that when you play a G chord, the G note would be in the bass. In this chapter, we'll explore *chord inversions* and how they are notated.

The definition of inversion is "to reverse the order or position of something." In our case, we will be changing the order of notes in a chord. The notes of a C chord would typically be voiced by stacking the C, E, and G notes, where C, being the root, would naturally be the bass note. When you invert this chord, you play the 3rd scale degree in the bass. In this case, that would be E.

 **NEW CHORD:** $\frac{1}{3}$

In the key of C, this is how it would be written in standard notation:

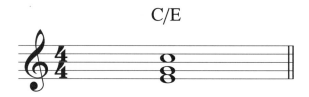

In our number chart, the chord would be notated like this: $\frac{1}{3}$

This is how the $\frac{1}{3}$ chord sounds in a musical phrase:

TRACK 49

Example S

1      $\frac{1}{3}$ 4   5   ⌢
                                     1

Caution: This chord is very similar to a 3-. In the key of C, the $\frac{1}{3}$ has the notes E, G, and **C**, while the 3- is voiced E, G, and **B**. They are close, but if you listen, you can hear the difference.

TRACK 50

Example T

1      $\frac{1}{3}$ 1   3-   ⌢
                                      ◇1◇

The Push

Thus far, all of the chord changes have been made on either beats one, two, three, or four. Now we are going to learn how to place chord changes in between the main pulses. To find the "beats between the beats," we need to learn how to *subdivide* the beat when we count it.

When we subdivide, we break the beat down into smaller parts. Here is how you would verbalize the count using a *quarter-note* pulse: "one–two–three–four."

When we subdivide to an *eighth-note* pulse, the count becomes: "one–&–two–&–three–&–four–&."

The *push* (<) allows us to place notes on the upbeats or "&" of a given beat.

As we already know, a single number standing alone represents a chord that will be played on beat one of the measure.

Placing a push over the top left of a number means that the chord is to be attacked an eighth note earlier, which in this case would be the "&" of beat four of the previous measure.

$$\overset{<}{5} \quad = \quad$$

In example U, you will hear the phrase played straight for the first four bars. The second phrase contains the same chords, but now all of the chords are pushed.

Example U

$$1 \qquad 5 \qquad \flat 7 \qquad 4$$
$$\overset{<}{1} \qquad \overset{<}{5} \qquad \overset{<}{\flat 7} \qquad \overset{<}{4} \qquad \boxed{\diamondsuit 1}$$

Notice how playing the chord on the "&" of beat four propelled the phrase forward. You will find the push to be very common in all styles and, thus, an extremely useful shorthand.

While the eighth-note push is a universally-accepted shorthand in the Number System world, there is not a universally-accepted shorthand for a *sixteenth-note push*. Some of my colleagues agree this is the best way to notate this rhythm.

$$\overset{<<}{5} \quad = \quad$$

Here is how that would sound:

Example V

$$1 \qquad \overset{<<}{\underset{3}{1}} \qquad 4 \qquad \overset{<<}{2-} \qquad \boxed{\diamondsuit 1}$$

Example Six

As we add more symbols and chords to our vocabulary, it will make our dictation examples more and more difficult. Be patient! Listen to the examples as many times as you need to get it right. The more you do this, the better you will get.

TRACK 53

_ _ _ _ _ _   _ _ _ _ _ _   _ _ _ _ _ _   _ _ _ _ _ _

_ _ _ _ _ _   _ _ _ _ _ _   _ _ _ _ _ _   _ _ _ _ _ _   _ _ _ _ _ _

1st and 2nd Endings, Tied Notes

In the last chapter, we learned about repeat signs. Very often, when an entire section is repeated, there is a slight variation towards the end of the repeat. In this case, we can use *1st and 2nd endings* to notate the variation. This shorthand is employed on our next chart. After playing the intro, verse, and chorus, play the first ending, then take the repeat back to the intro. Once you have played down to where the first ending begins, you skip over it and play the second ending in its place. Using this notation saves a ton of time writing the chart and makes the chart shorter and easier to understand.

This chart also introduces the use of a *tie*. When a tie (⌒) is bridged between two measures, it tells the player to not re-attack the chord. Instead, you continue to hold the chord from the previous measure.

Suspended ♯4th Chord

OK, this is not a typical chord, but it is the voicing used by the guitar and piano in our next song. You can hear it played on beat one of measure five of the verse. It is played in the same manner as the sus4 chord, only you are suspending a ♯4 instead. The Bsus♯4 is played B, E♯ (also known as F), and F♯. You can also invert the voicing by playing F♯, B, E♯. Either way, it is resolved by moving the E♯ note down to D♯. The first measure of the piece alternates between a 1 chord and a 1maj7 chord. Why do I not put these chords on the chart? It's a judgment call. The bass and drums do not play the push that you would have to write and I think it would just clutter up the page. This is a good reason to keep your ears open. It is a part of being a guitar player to have to listen and copy. Besides, if I can play it on guitar, then it must be easy!

TRACKS 54-58

One More Minute with You

This next song is a driving pop/rock song. Watch out for the ♭3 chord in the chorus and the ♭6 chord in the bridge. This song is in the key of F♯, so the ♭3 is an A major chord, and the ♭6 is a D major chord. Remember bass players, you play the bottom note on these inverted chords. In this song, the $\frac{1}{3}$ chord has you playing A♯. That means you have an A♯ and an A to play in the same chorus, so pay close attention!

Recorded with a female vocal in the key of F♯. Suggested male key: B.

POP-ROCK ♩ = 140

ONE MORE MINUTE WITH YOU

I) 1x GUITAR ONLY

‖: 1   1   1   1   2x (CRASH ♪ ♩ ♫ ♩)

V) 1   1   1   1   (HI-HAT ♪ ♩ ♫ ♩)

4   4   4   4

1   1   1   1

4   4   4   4

CHA) FULL BAND

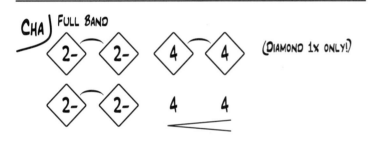

(DIAMOND 1x ONLY!)

CH) 1   5   ⅓   4   1x (CRASH ♪ ♩ ♫ ♩)   2x (CRASH ♫ ♩ ♫ ♩)

1   5   [1. b3 ◇4 :‖] [2. b3   4]

CH) <1   5   ⅓   4

1   5   b3   4

BR)   R.H. ON FLOOR TOM. (♫ ♩ ♫ ♩)

b6   b6   b7   b7

1   1

b6   b6   b7   b7

4   4   b3   4   <

SOLO) 1   5   ⅓   4   (CRASH ♫ ♩. ♫ ♩)

1   5   b3   4

CH) 1   5   ^⅓   ✗   (CRASH ♫ ♩ ♫ ♩)

<1   5   b3   4

CH) <1   5   ⅓   4   (CRASH ♫ ♩ ♫ ♩)

1   5   b3   4   <

OUT) ‖: 1   5   ⅓   4   (CRASH ♫ ♩ ♫ ♩)

1   5   b3   4   :‖ ◇1◠

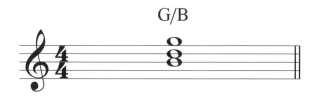

$\frac{5}{7}$ Chords, Short Bars

 **NEW CHORD:** $\frac{5}{7}$

As we learned in Chapter Six, the top number of an inversion tells us what chord to play, and the bottom number tells us the bass note. In the key of C, the $\frac{5}{7}$ would be a G chord with B in the bass. Since this is still a new concept, let me break down how I got there. In the key of C, C=1, D=2, E=3, F=4 and G=5, so G is our 5 chord. Now I continue to count up to find the bass note: A=6 and B=7, so B is our bass note.

This is how it would be written in traditional notation.

G/B

The $\frac{5}{7}$ chord is very handy as a *passing chord* between the 1 chord and the 6- chord. When we use the $\frac{1}{3}$ chord in the same fashion, we can walk all the way down the scale:

Example W

1	$\frac{5}{7}$	6-	5
4	$\frac{1}{3}$	2-	1

In fact, if you take a closer look, you will see that both the $\frac{1}{3}$ and the $\frac{5}{7}$ chords are *first inversion chords* (which means that the 3rd of the chord is holding down the bass). This is important to recognize because, for example, a C chord with an E in the bass is a $\frac{1}{3}$ in the key of C, but the same chord functions as a $\frac{5}{7}$ in the key of F. Examples of some other first inversion chords would be $\frac{4}{6}$, $\frac{3}{5}$, and $\frac{2}{4}$, you get the idea.

NEW CONCEPT: ## Short Bars

Popular music generally stays in the same time signature throughout the song. However, it is very common to see a measure of a different time signature interjected into a composition to disrupt the otherwise even flow of the music. The most common short bar is 2/4 time. Where a measure in 4/4 time has four beats, a measure in 2/4 time only has two. All short bars are placed in parentheses. The number of beats that it takes up depends on how many dots are over the measure.

Here is how a 2/4 measure would be written:

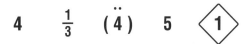

Here is a musical phrase employing short bar notation:

TRACK 60

Example X

The same musical phrase can be written and performed with a bar of 3/4 time. 3/4 time has three beats per measure, so you will place three dots over the short measure.

TRACK 61

Example Y

$$4 \qquad \frac{1}{3} \qquad (\overset{\cdots}{4}) \qquad 5 \qquad \langle 1 \rangle$$

Author's note: There is a common practice of placing a time signature inside the brackets instead of using dots over it. The problem with this is that the 2/4 time signature can be easily mistaken for a 2 chord with a 4 in the bass. Therefore, I recommend using the dots; however, you should be aware that many people use the time signature inside the brackets instead of the dots.

✏ DICTATION:

Example Seven

This example, of course, will include a short bar, so keep your ears open.

A little hint: There are no split bars contained in this example, so listen for the chord that gets played for a shorter duration than the rest. Count how many beats it is played for, parenthesize it, and dot it up!

TRACK 62

_____   _____   _____   _____

_____   _____   _____   _____

_____   _____   _____   _____

6/8 Time

Up until now, all of our music has been in 4/4 time. Our new time signature is *6/8 time*. 6/8 means that there are six beats per measure with the eighth-note pulse representing each beat. Even though there are six separate beats, 6/8 time is usually felt as two groups of three.

$$1–2–3–4–5–6$$

In 6/8 time, a number standing alone would still represent the entire measure. When a split bar is used, it should be understood that the first chord would be played on beat one and you would change chords on beat four. In standard notation, you would place the time signature to the left of the first measure. Since time signatures are written as fractions and so are inverted chords, I find it best to put time signature information up in the right-hand corner with the tempo and feel of the song.

 **CHORD SPOTLIGHT:**

Add9 Chord

This chord is pretty self explanatory. You play a major triad and simply "add" the 9th (counting up from the root of the chord) onto the top of the chord. A B♭add9 chord is voiced B♭–D–F–C. This chord should be distinguished from the add2 chord, which uses the same notes but stacks them B♭–C–D–F.

TRACKS 63-67

The Gift

This next song is in 6/8 time with a pop ballad feel. It features a short bar at the end of the solo going into the last chorus. Since each regular measure in this song has six beats, our short measure will have three. You may think that one short measure in the entire song is a rather sparse use of our new concept, but in fact, this is typical of the way that it is commonly used.

Recorded with a male vocal in the key of C. Suggested female key: F.

KEY OF C $\frac{6}{8}$ POP BALLAD ♩. = 60

THE GIFT

I)
1	$\frac{5}{7}$	$\frac{1}{3}$	4	(RIDE ♩ ♪♩ ♪)
1	$\frac{5}{7}$	$\frac{1}{3}$	◇4◇ ◇4◇	

SOLO)
1	5	$\frac{1}{3}$	4	(RIDE ♩ ♪♩ ♪)
6-	5	$\frac{1}{3}$	4	(4)

V) HI-HAT & SIDE STICK 1x, HI-HAT & SNARE 2x (♩. 𝄽 ♪♩. 𝄽.)

‖: 6-	4	1	5
6-	4	1	5
$\frac{1}{3}$	4	1	5
$\frac{1}{3}$	4	$\frac{1}{3}$ 1	5

CH)
X 1	$\frac{5}{7}$	$\frac{1}{3}$	4	(RIDE ♩ ♪♩ ♪)
1	$\frac{5}{7}$	$\frac{1}{3}$	4	
6- 5 4		6- 5 4		
6- 5 2-		◇4◇ ◇4◇		

CH)
1	$\frac{5}{7}$	$\frac{1}{3}$	4	(RIDE ♩ ♪♩ ♪)
1	$\frac{5}{7}$	$\frac{1}{3}$	4	
6- 5 4		6- 5 2-	(1x ONLY) ◇4◇	

1.
| 1 | $\frac{5}{7}$ | $\frac{1}{3}$ | 4 | :‖ |

2.
1	1

OUT)
‖: 1	$\frac{5}{7}$	$\frac{1}{3}$	4	(RIDE ♩ ♪♩ ♪)
1	$\frac{5}{7}$	$\frac{1}{3}$	4	:‖ 🝔 ◇1◇

BR)
♭7ADD9	$\frac{4}{6}$	1	$\frac{5}{7}$	(RIDE ♩ ♪♩ ♪)
♭7ADD9	$\frac{4}{6}$	1	1	
♭7ADD9	$\frac{4}{6}$	1	$\frac{5}{7}$	
2-	4	5SUS4	5	

CHAPTER EIGHT:

$\frac{1}{5}$ Chords, Pedal Notes

$\frac{1}{5}$

Over the last two chapters, we introduced the first inversion chord where the 3rd of the triad is played as the bass note. Our newest chord is a *second inversion* chord where the 5th scale degree is in the bass. In the key of F, the 1 chord is F–A–C. Taking the 5th scale degree (C) and putting it in the bass would be written in traditional notation like this:

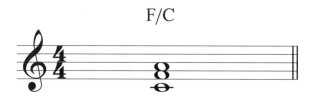

F/C

 Here is what a $\frac{1}{5}$ sounds like in the context of the musical phrase:

TRACK 68

Example Z

4   1 $\frac{1}{5}$ 5   ⟨1⟩

This chord is frequently used as a dramatic setup to the 5 chord, but can also be used as a substitution for a regular 5 chord by the songwriter. The $\frac{1}{5}$ is by far the most common second inversion chord, but they are as abundant as root position chords.

💡 **NEW CONCEPT:**

Pedal Notes

Sometimes for dramatic effect during a series of chord changes, the bass note can be left unchanged (*pedal note*), causing musical tension throughout the section. This is because when you are pedaling the bass note, it may or may not actually be part of the chord. This would be notated in the same way as inversions: chord on top, bass note on bottom.

Here is a musical passage demonstrating the concept of pedal notes.

TRACK 69

Example AA

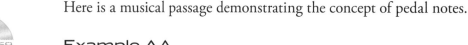

1    $\frac{4}{1}$ $\frac{5}{1}$ $\frac{4}{1}$ ⟨1⟩

The chords are basically 1–4–5–4–1, but the bass note never strays from the 1 chord. This is another creative musical tool for charting as well as composing.

DICTATION:

TRACK 70

Example Eight

Listening to how the bass line is moving (or not moving) will be the key to getting this one right. If you establish that the bass is staying the same, write the pedal notes in on your first listen, then fill in the chords above on the second.

_ _ _ _ _ _ _   _ _ _ _ _ _ _   _ _ _ _ _ _   _ _ _ _ _ _

_ _ _ _ _ _ _   _ _ _ _ _ _ _   _ _ _ _ _ _ _   _ _ _ _ _ _ _   _ _ _ _ _ _ _

CHART TOOLS:

TRACKS 71-75

Half-time Feel and Forte-Piano

Sometimes a writer will break up the monotony of a steady groove by writing one section of the piece in *half-time feel*. In the case of our next song, that will be the bridge. When you get to the bridge, the groove that was taking one measure to play will now take two. The speed at which the measures pass by, however, will remain the same. I would recommend listening to the full arrangement track before jumping into the "minus you" track in order to make sure that you fully understand this concept.

We will also be using the dynamic marking *fp*, which stands for *forte-piano*. This indicates that you play a loud note followed immediately by a soft one—a great dramatic effect.

Feeling's Gone

This is a high-energy, pop-rock song with plenty of eighties retro flair. It features some less common chords, so make sure you are ready for them before you begin the play-along. The bridge goes into half-time, and eight measures into the bridge, the song pedals on the 1 while the chords change above. Also, pay attention to the sixteenth-note build up at the end of the bridge.

Recorded with a female vocal in the key of E. Suggested male key: A.

FEELING'S GONE

I) DRUM INTRO — (CRASH ♫ ♩ ♫ ♩)

X   X

1	b6	b3	b7
1	b6	b3	b7

||: 1   1

V) — (HI-HAT ♫ ♩ ♪ ♪ ♩)

1	1	5	5
b7	b7	4	4
1	1	5	5
b7	b7	4	4
b3	4	1	1
b3	4	b6	b7

CH) — (CRASH ♫ ♩ ♫ ♩)

1	b6	b3	b7	
1	b6	b3	b7	:||
1	b6	b3	b7	
1	b6	b3	b7	

◇1◇ — ◇1◇

BR) HALF-TIME — (RIDE ♩ 𝄾 ♩ 𝄾 | ♩ ♩ ♩ 𝄾)

1/5	b6	b3/5	b7/4
1/5	b6	b3/5	b7

1	b6/1	b3/1	b7/1	(♫ ♫ →)

fp

1	b6/1	b3/1	b7/1	(♬ →)

fp

CH) END HALF-TIME — (CRASH ♫ ♩ ♫ ♩)

1	b6	b3	b7
1	b6	b3	b7

CH)

1	b6	b3	b7
1	b6	b3	b7

OUT) — (CRASH ♩ ♫ ♫ ♩)

1	1	1	1	^1

CHAPTER NINE:

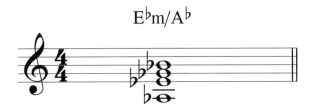 Chords, Key Changes

 **NEW CHORD:** $\frac{4\text{-}}{\flat7}$

In Chapter Eight, we touched on the concept of playing a bass note that is not part of the original chord. One of my favorite examples of this is a 4- chord with a $\flat$7 in the bass. In the key of B$\flat$, the 4- chord is E$\flat$ minor (voiced E$\flat$–G$\flat$–B$\flat$), and the $\flat$7 note is A$\flat$. Here's what that looks like in standard notation.

E$\flat$m/A$\flat$

 Here is a phrase using our new $\frac{4\text{-}}{\flat7}$ chord:

Example BB

1    $\frac{1}{3}$ 4 $\frac{4\text{-}}{\flat7}$ ◇1◇

This of course, opens up a whole new world of adventurous and sometimes demented possibilities as far as bass notes are concerned. This becomes extremely helpful for charting songs that were written on piano where the bass-note voicings can be more complex.

 NEW CONCEPT: ## Key Change

It is somewhat common for a song to change keys in the middle or towards the end. This is referred to as a *modulation*, or *mod* for short. Notating a modulation in this system is incredibly simple. You write your chart as usual and, at the point where you want to modulate, you simply write the name of the new key. Here is an example where the first line is in the key of B$\flat$, and the second line then changes to the key of C.

Example CC

Key of B$\flat$
1   5   2-   <u>4   5</u>
Key of C
1   5   2-   <u>4   5</u>
◇1◇

This type of notation makes it easy to read and understand the modulation because, unlike letter names, the numbers will continue to show you the function of the chord. Once you establish the modulation to a new key, you will remain in that key for the rest of the song or until another key is established.

DICTATION:

TRACK 78

Example Nine

The two things to look out for are the new $\frac{4}{\flat7}$ chord and the modulation. I can tell you we are starting in the key of B♭. You need to notate where the mod begins as well as what key we are going to.

Key of B♭: _ _ _ _ _ _   _ _ _ _ _ _   _ _ _ _ _ _   _ _ _ _ _ _

_ _ _ _ _ _   _ _ _ _ _ _

Key of ___: _ _ _ _ _ _   _ _ _ _ _ _   _ _ _ _ _ _   _ _ _ _ _ _

_ _ _ _ _ _

 **CHART TOOLS:**

Tempo Variations

These are borrowed directly from standard notation. The first is *rit.*, which is short for *ritardando*. This Italian word means, "becoming gradually slower." It is frequently used at the end of songs for dramatic effect and is notated under the line of music with the abbreviation rit. and a series of dots. The idea is to slow down starting from the rit. and continue to slow down for the duration of the dots to the desired tempo, or, in most cases, to the end of the song.

The second is *accel.* which is short for *accelerando*. It means, as the name would imply, "becoming gradually faster." It is notated in the exact same manner as *ritardando*. Much less common than *ritardando*, *accelerando* might be used in a musical medley where you are trying to transition to a faster tempo.

 **CHORD SPOTLIGHT:**

Augmented, Dominant 9th, and Minor 7th

An *augmented chord* is built entirely of major 3rd intervals. Play a D major triad (D–F♯–A), raise the 5th by a half step (A to A♯), and you have D+ (D augmented).

There are so many variations of 9th chords that I find it more effective to be very specific about what you want. To make a dominant 9th chord (an A♭9 chord appears in "My Life Without You"), we start with a dominant seventh chord (A♭7: A♭–C–E♭–G♭), place our 9th (B♭) on top, and we have ourselves a thick chord. In an effort to "thin" the voicing out, it is not uncommon to actually drop the root of the chord, which leaves us with C–E♭–G♭–B♭.

A minor 7th chord is a very popular chord in many styles. It's built by adding a ♭7th on top of a minor triad. A Dm7 would be voiced D–F–A–C.

TRACKS 79-83

My Life Without You

This is a retro ballad and a tribute to the greatest four-piece band of the last century. As you would expect, this song uses our new $\frac{4}{\flat7}$ chord, a key change that occurs after the bridge, and a slight rit. at the end of the piece.

Recorded with a male vocal in the key of C♯. Suggested female key: B.

MY LIFE WITHOUT YOU

I) PIANO ONLY

1   1

V) DRUMS 2X ONLY
$$\left(\,♩\ ♩\ \sqcap\ ♩\, \right)$$

‖: 1   1ᴹᴬᴶ7   4   4- $\frac{4-}{♭7}$

1   1ᴹᴬᴶ7   4 $\frac{4-}{♭7}$

GUITAR & BASS ENTER

2- ♭2+ $\frac{4}{1}$ $\frac{5^9}{7}$ 2- ♭2+ $\frac{4}{1}$ 5

CH) DRUMS 2X ONLY
RIDE
$$\left(\,♩\ ♩\ \sqcap\ ♩\, \right)$$

6-7   4ᴹᴬᴶ7   1⁹ 1 $\frac{5}{7}$

6-7   4ᴹᴬᴶ7   1⁹ 1 $\frac{5}{7}$

♭6   4- $\frac{4-}{♭7}$ 1 1ˢᵘˢ⁴ ⟨1⟩   [1.] :‖ [2.] 1

BR)

5   6- 5   4 $\frac{1}{3}$ 2- 1
RIDE
$$\left(\,♩\ ♩\ \sqcap\ ♩\, \right)$$

5   6- 5 $\frac{2}{\sharp4}$ 5ˢᵘˢ⁴   ⟨5⟩

V) KEY OF E♭
RIDE
$$\left(\,♩\ ♩\ \sqcap\ ♩\, \right)$$

‖: 1   1ᴹᴬᴶ7   4   4- $\frac{4-}{♭7}$

1   1ᴹᴬᴶ7   4   [1.] 5ˢᵘˢ⁴ 5 :‖ [2.] 5ˢᵘˢ⁴ 5 ⟨1⟩

RIT.....................

CHAPTER TEN:
Integrating Standard Notation into Number Charts, The "1" Method

 **NEW CONCEPT:**

Integrating Standard Notation

Every once in a while, you will come across a rhythm that is too *syncopated* for Number System shorthand. In this case, I always find it best to slip a little bit of *standard rhythmic notation* into the number charts. There are two types of situations in which you can insert standard notation into your chart. The first is where the rhythm is complicated, but the note remains the same. In this instance, I would recommend writing the rhythm under the chord and underlining the entire measure as you would a split bar.

TRACK 84
MP³

Example DD

4   4   1

The next situation would be when the rhythm is complicated, and the notes are changing. Here you notate the rhythm and write the chords under the corresponding rhythm, once again underlining the entire measure. For this example, the syncopated rhythm is single notes, but at a slower tempo, you could notate chords this way.

TRACK 85
MP³

Example EE

♭6   ♭7

If you do not know how to read standard notation, I highly recommended that you learn. There are books written for your instrument that will start you out with the most basic notation. I have also included some reference materials on standard notation in the back of the book.

I deliberately waited until the end of the book to introduce this next concept. You may know that I am a drummer. Some people would say, "What use is the Number System to a drummer? Of what benefit is it to the drummer to know what chords are coming up? He won't be playing them." My response is this: Knowing what chords are coming up affects what I decide to play as a drummer. If a song has been filled with a bunch of 1–4–5 type changes and the bridge is starting on a ♭7, there is going to be a dramatic change in harmony and I'm going to want to set it up that way. Besides, if you do not understand the language of numbers that the rest of the band is using then you are putting yourself at a disadvantage. Having said all of that, there are many fine drummers that do not read numbers, but are able to use this system's rhythmic concepts. "How," you ask?

The "1" Method (For Drummers Only)

The "1" method is where, instead of writing down each of the chords, you mark down a 1 in its place. You won't have the chordal information, but you still have all of the phrasing, pushes, diamonds, and stops that you would have on a typical number chart. Let me show you:

Example FF

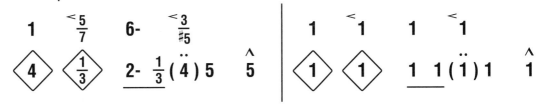

Notice how the charts side by side are identical except that the 1s are being substituted for the chord numbers. You might ask why I bothered to notate the split bar since we are not charting the chords. The answer is, as we learned in Chapter Three, a split bar implies accents on beats one and three, and as the drummer, you want to know that. It is very important that you include all of the rhythmic notation that you would see in a regular chord chart to give yourself the best chance to perform the music accurately. While it is a valuable asset as a drummer to be able to read a number chart that has been handed to you, the "1" method is an extremely fast way for the drummer who may be slow with chord recognition to write out their own effective chart.

Example Ten

In this exercise, we are going to write a chart using the "1" method. Pay close attention to the phrasing as well as any pushes, diamonds, marcatos, etc. If you hear a syncopated rhythm that cannot be charted using the Number System's rhythmic notation, then "bail out" and write a bar of standard rhythmic notation.

-------   -------   -------   -------

-------   -------   -------   -------

-------   -------   -------   -------

-------   -------   -------   -------   -------

Measure Repeat Sign

This symbol (✗) borrowed from standard notation that tells you to repeat the previous measure. I tend to use this symbol to facilitate the repeat of a complicated rhythm.

Before

The last tune is a pop-metal song. It starts with a riff that is notated with our new integrated rhythmic system. It is also noteworthy to point out that this song is in a minor key. Before you play through this chart, take a closer look at those measures with standard notation and work out the licks.

Recorded with a female vocal in the key of E. Suggested male key: G.

BEFORE

I) KEYS ONLY

⟨1⟩ ⟨1⟩

SINGLE NOTES (GUITAR ENTERS)
1 ♭9 ♭9 ♭7 1   1 ♭9 ♭9 ♭7 1 4 3 1

POWER CHORDS (BAND ENTERS) (HI-HAT)
1 ♭2 ♭2 ♭7 1   1 ♭2 ♭2 ♭7 1 4 3 1

(RIDE)

1-   5-   ♭3   4

1-   5-   ♭3   4

V) (HI-HAT)
1-   5-   ♭3   4

1-   5-   ♭3   ⁝4̈ ♭2̇

(HI-HAT)
1-   5-   ♭3   4

1-   5-   ♭3   ⟨4⟩ ⟨4⟩ ♭2̇

CH) (RIDE)
1-   ♭3   ♭7   4

1-   ♭3   ♭7   4

1.
1   1

2.
1-   1-
fp <

BR) (CRASH)
♭6   ♭7   1-   ♭3

♭6   ♭7   (SINGLE NOTES)
1 ♭2 ♭2 ♭7 1   1 2 4 ♭3

♭6   ♭7   1-   ♭3

♭6   ♭7   ⟨1⟩ ⟨1⟩ ⟨1⟩ ⟨1⟩

I) KEYS PEDAL 1. BASS & DRUMS OUT 1x
1 ♭9 ♭9 ♭7 1   1 ♭9 ♭9 ♭7 1 4 3 1

1 ♭9 ♭9 ♭7 1   1.   ✗   ⁝

2.   1-

SOLO) (RIDE)
1-   ♭3   ♭7   4

1-   ♭3   ♭7   4̂

CH)
♭7 1 ♭3   ♭7   4

1-   ♭3   ♭7   4

CH)
1-   ♭3   ♭7   4

1-   ♭3   ♭7   4

OUT)
1   ％   1̂

BEFORE ("1" METHOD)

Final Thoughts

Keep in mind that the Number System to this point is not standardized among all professional musicians. Those of you who find yourselves in a Nashville session will notice slight variations in each leader's charting method. I hope you find this charting system as useful in your career as I have in mine. My hope is that you will share this information with your fellow musicians in the hope that this system can benefit working musicians and music students worldwide. For continued information on this system, please visit **www.thenashvillenumbersystem.com**.

Anatomy of a Chart:
How to Write a Number Chart That Everyone Can Read

Over the years, I have seen many minor variations in writing number charts. What I am presenting here is what I believe to be the most concise way to format your chart so that everyone understands what they need to do.

First, put the title of the song at the top of the page. To the left of the title, I generally put the key of the song (although that can be easily changed), and to the right, I may put the feel of the song and/or the tempo. Also, if the time signature is something other than 4/4, you can write that in as well.

As you begin to write your chart, leave a small margin to the left of the numbers. This is where you will put your section markers such as the verse and intro. As you are writing the chart, pay close attention to the phrasing. As a new phrase starts (generally every four measures), start a new line. Try to keep your growing column of phrases on the left side of the page. You will find out why soon. Phrases group together to form sections. As you enter a new section, draw a horizontal line between the sections and clearly label each one.

As you get to the bottom of the page, draw a line down the middle, starting under the title, and start a second column down the right-hand side of the page. Remember to leave room to the left of the new dividing line for the section markers.

A note to drummers: Use the space in the margins to write out the groove that you will be using for each section. You will generally have one groove that you use for each section, so write a sample bar in parentheses, so you remember what you need to play.

Answers to Dictation Examples

Example One

1   4   5   4

1   5   1

Example Two

1   5   6-   4

1   5   ◇4◇   ◇5◇   ◇1◇

Example Three

1   5   <u>4 1</u>   <u>4 5</u>   ⌢

6-   5   4   <u>2- 5</u>   ◇1◇

Example Four

                                ⌢

<u>$\overset{\cdots}{1}$ $\overset{\cdot}{5}$4   5 $6\text{-}\overset{\cdots}{5}$ $6\text{-}{}^{\flat}7$ 4</u>   ◇1◇

Example Five

$\overset{\wedge}{1}$ 3-   4   5

$\overset{\wedge}{6\text{-}}$ $\overset{\wedge}{3\text{-}}$ 2-   4   ⌢ ◇1◇

Example Six

1   5 $\frac{1}{3}$ 4

$\overset{<}{6\text{-}}$ $\overset{<}{5}$ $\frac{1}{3}$ $\overset{<}{4}$ ⌢ ◇1◇

Example Seven

1      $\overset{<}{5}$ ♭7 $\overset{<}{4}$

5   6-   ♭7 $(\overset{\cdots}{\frac{5}{7}})$ ⌢

1   4   1   5   ◇6-◇

Example Eight

1      $\frac{4}{1}$ $\frac{5}{1}$ $\frac{4}{1}$ ⌢

1   4 $\frac{1}{5}$ 5   ◇1◇

Example Nine

KEY OF B♭

1   6-   4 $\frac{4\text{-}}{\flat 7}$

1   ◇1◇

KEY OF C

1      $\frac{1}{3}$ 4 $\frac{4\text{-}}{\flat 7}$ ⌢ ◇1◇

Example Ten

◇1◇   ◇1◇   ◇1◇   ◇1◇

1   1   1   ♩. ♪ ♩ ♩

1      $\overset{<}{1}$ 1 $\overset{<}{1}$

1      $\overset{<}{1}$ 1   1 $\overset{\wedge}{1}$

Glossary

Accidentals: The name given to refer to *sharps* and *flats* as a whole.

Accel.: See *Accelerando.*

Accelerando (*ah-chel-le-RAHN-do*)**:** Italian word meaning "gradually get faster." Typically notated with the abbreviation, *accel.*, followed by dots, indicating its duration.

Augmented: Raised or enlarged.

Augmented chord: Three-note *triad* using the *root, 3rd,* and *augmented* (raised) *5th.*

Augmented fourth: See *interval.*

Augmented fifth: See *interval.*

Bass clef (𝄢): Symbol used on the musical *staff* denoting the following note-to-staff assignments:

Used by instruments like the bass guitar and the left hand of the keyboard to read *notes* in a lower register than those reading the *treble clef.*

Beat: Rhythmic unit of time.

Br: Abbreviation for "bridge." See *bridge.*

Breakdown: *Number System* term implying particularly sparse and quiet treatment of the prescribed section.

Bridge: Transitional part of the *song.* It is typically abbreviated as *Br.* Unlike the *verse* or *chorus*, the section is rarely repeated within the song structure.

Ch: Abbreviation for "chorus." See *chorus.*

Cha: Abbreviation for "channel." See *channel.*

Channel: Short subsection of a *song* that directly precedes and musically sets up the *chorus.* The *channel* is considered part of the *verse*, but its *chord* structure is unlike the rest of the verse. While most every song has a verse, not every song has a channel. Sometimes referred to as *pre-chorus.*

Chart: Visual representation of a *song* as written using the *Number System.*

Chord: Group of at least three *notes* played simultaneously.

Chord inversions: *Chord* whose lowest played *note* is other than the *root.* A first inversion chord is typically stacked using the 3rd on the bottom, 5th in the middle, and the root on top. The second inversion chord is typically stacked using the 5th on the bottom, the root in the middle, and the 3rd on top.

Chord numbers: When playing in any given *key*, there are 12 possible *roots* for *chords.*

Chord quality: Refers to the type of *chord* being played. Some choices for *chord quality* are *major, minor, augmented,* and *diminished.*

Chromatic scale: Twelve-note *scale* consisting of *half steps.*

Chorus: Repeated section of a *song*, sometimes referred to as the refrain. It is typically abbreviated as *Ch.* Generally, most or all of the words in this section remain the same throughout the song.

Common time: Nickname given to the *4/4 time signature* due to it being the most common time signature in musical history. See *4/4 time.*

Cresc.: See *crescendo.*

Crescendo (*krec-SHEN-doh*): Italian word meaning "gradually get louder." It can be notated with the abbreviation *cresc.* followed by dots indicating its duration, or with ⟨ .

Decrescendo (*deh-kresh-SHEN-doh*): Italian word meaning "gradually get softer." It is typically notated with ⟩ .

Diamond (◇): *Number System* symbol that, when drawn around a *chord* number, tells the player to stop playing *rhythm* and play that chord as a *whole note.* ⟨1⟩ = ○

Diminish: To make smaller.

Diminished chord: *Chord* made up entirely of stacked *minor thirds.* The symbol for this chord is a small circle to the upper right of the *chord number* (°). In the *number system*, it is usually implied that a *diminished chord* is a *diminished* seventh chord.

DO (*doh*): *Solfege* syllable meaning the first or *root* note of the *scale.* Synonymous with 1 in the *Number System.*

Double-time feel: Term used to denote where the groove is played twice as fast as the previous section. In a double-time section, a groove that took an entire bar to play would be played twice each bar. Please note that the speed at which the bars pass does not change.

Dynamics: The degree of loudness or softness at which the music should be played. The *dynamic* markings from softest to loudest are: *pp*, *p*, *mp*, *mf*, *f*, and *ff*.

Eighth note (♪): A *note* half the length of a *quarter note*, and an eighth the length of a *whole note.* The subdivision of the *eighth note* is vocalized as follows: "1–&–2–&–3–&–4–&." See "Note Values and Relationships."

Eighth rest (𝄾): Holds the same duration as the *eighth note*; the *eighth rest* tells you to rest, or not play, for that duration.

𝒇 : See *forte.*

FA (*fah*): *Solfege* syllable representing the 4th *scale degree.* Synonymous with 4 in the *Number System.*

Fermata (*fehr-Mah-tah*): Italian term meaning "to hold." When a player sees this symbol, ⌢, above a number or *note*, they are to hold out the current *chord* until cut off by the leader or director.

𝒇𝒇 : See *fortissimo.*

First ending: Bracketed section of a *song*, directly preceding a *repeat sign*, that is only played the first time through.

⌐1̄‾‾‾‾‾¬
57

First inversion chord: See *chord inversions.*

Flat (♭): Symbol that, when placed next to any number or *note*, lowers its pitch by a *half step.*

Form: The structure of a *song* as described by its individual sections. Typical pop *form* might be *intro–verse–chorus–turnaround–verse–chorus–bridge–solo–chorus–outo.*

Forte (*FOUR-tay*): Italian word meaning "loud." This *dynamic* marking is abbreviated as *f*.

Forte-Piano (*four-tay PIA-noh*): *Dynamic* indication of Italian origin instructing the player to play one loud *note*, immediately followed by soft ones. This *dynamic* marking is abbreviated as *fp*.

Fortissimo (*four-TEE-see-moe*): Italian word meaning "very loud." This *dynamic* marking is abbreviated as *ff*.

4/4 Time: *Time signature* with four *beats* per *measure* using the *quarter note* to represent one beat. Also referred to as *common time.*

fp: See *forte-piano*.

Grand staff: Combination of the *treble clef* and *bass clef* used mostly by keyboard players.

Half note (♩): A *note* equal in value to two *quarter notes* and half the value of a *whole note*. See section on "Note Values and Relationships."

Half rest (➖): Holds the same duration as the *half note*; the *half rest* tells you to rest, or not play, for that duration. See section on "Note Values and Relationships."

Half step: Smallest *interval* in western music. Two *half steps* equal a *whole step*, and there are 12 half steps in an *octave*.

Half-time feel: Term used to denote a section of *song* where the groove is played half as fast as the previous section. In *half-time feel*, a groove that took one *measure* to play would now take two measures. Please note that the speed at which the measures pass does not change.

I: abbreviation for "Intro." See *intro*.

Interval: The distance between two *notes*. The different types are minor (m), major (M), perfect (P), augmented (A), and diminished (D). In C, the intervals from smallest to largest are:

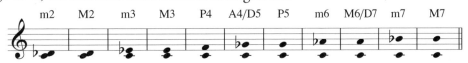

Intro: Short for "introduction." Represents the section at the beginning of a *song* that precedes the *verse*.

Key: The tonal *root* of a *song*. The *key* of the song would be represented by the 1 *chord*.

Key signature: In *standard notation*, a *key signature* is a series of *sharps* or *flats* placed on the *staff*, designating *notes* that are to be consistently played one *half step* higher or lower unless otherwise altered with an *accidental*.

LA: *Solfege* syllable representing the 6th *scale degree*. Synonymous with 6 in the *Number System*.

Major chord: Three-note *chord* that includes the *root*, *major third*, and *perfect fifth*. Chords are assumed major in the *Number System* unless otherwise notated.

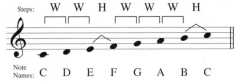

Major fourth: See *interval*.

Major scale: Progression of *notes* using the following steps from the *root note*: *whole–whole–half–whole–whole–whole–half*. The basis of the *Number System* uses numbers for the degrees of the *major scale*. In C:

Major second: See *interval*.

Major seventh: See *interval*.

Major seventh chord: A four-note *chord* created by adding a major 7th on top of a *major chord*. Cmaj7 would be spelled C–E–G–B.

Major sixth: See *interval*.

Marcato (^): *Standard notation* symbol applied to the *Number System*. If placed over a number (or *note*), it means to play one short note followed by rest for the duration of the note. (slang: rooftop).

Measure: A unit of time as defined by the *time signature*.

MI: *Solfege* syllable representing the 3rd *scale degree*. Synonymous with 3 in the *Number System*.

Minor chord: Three-note *chord* that consists of the *root*, *minor third*, and *perfect fifth*. In the *Number System*, a dash "-" is placed to the right of a number to designate it a *minor chord*. Example: "4-" equals a minor four chord.

Minor scale: Progression of *notes* using the following steps from the *root* note: *whole–half–whole–whole–half–whole–whole*. *Minor scales* can also be played starting from the 6th degree of any *major scale*. This is called the *relative minor*.

Minor seventh: See *interval*.

Minor sixth: See *interval*.

Minor third: See *interval*.

Mod: See *modulation*.

Modulation: To change the tonal center of a composition by reassigning the *root*, or 1 chord, to something other than the original *key*.

Nashville Number System: See *Number System*.

Note: 1. A symbol used in *standard musical notation* to represent the relative duration and pitch of a sound. 2. A sound with a definite pitch.

Number System: Shorthand musical notation adapted from Roman numeral analysis from the 1800s for use in popular music by Nashville musicians in the 1950s. It uses numbers to represent *scale degrees* and groups the numbers into *phrases* and sections. Also known as the Nashville *Number System*.

Octave: The *interval* between the 1st *scale degree* and the 8th scale degree. The *octave* is vibrating at a frequency twice that of the *root*. In other words, with an A vibrating at a frequency of 440 times per second, its octave is vibrating at 880 times per second.

Out: See *outro*.

Outro: The final section of *song*, usually performed instrumentally. The opposite of *intro*. This section is usually represented with the abbreviation, *out*.

𝒑: See *piano*.

Passing chord: *Chords* used in between *root-position* chords that facilitate stepwise motion of the bass line. Here's an example of a decending bass line using passing chords to fill in the harmony:

1	$\frac{5}{7}$	6-	5
4	$\frac{1}{3}$	2-	1

Pedal Note: Refers to the same bass *note* played under a series of changing *chords*.

Perfect fifth: See *interval*.

Perfect fourth: See *interval*.

Phrase: A complete musical idea that is a building block of the composition as a whole.

piano (*PIA-noh*): Italian word meaning "soft." This *dynamic* marking is abbreviated as *p*.

pianissimo (*pi-a-NEES-see-moh*): Italian word meaning "very soft." This *dynamic* marking is abbreviated as *pp*.

Pre-Chorus: See *Channel*.

Push (<): *Number System* symbol that, when placed above a *chord*, moves the attack of that chord back by one *eighth note*.

pp: See *pianissimo*.

Quarter note (♩): A *note* with a value and duration one-fourth that of a *whole note*. In *4/4 time*, it is the main pulse and counted "1——2——3——4." See "Note Values and Relationships."

Quarter rest (𝄽): Holds the same duration as the *quarter note*; the *quarter rest* tells you to rest, or not play, for that duration. See "Note Values and Relationships."

RE (*ray*): *Solfege* syllable representing the 2nd *scale degree*. Synonymous with 2 in the *Number System*.

Repeat sign (   ): A pair of symbols that tells you to repeat all material in between the repeat brackets one time unless otherwise notated.

Rest: An interval of silence in a piece of music, marked by a symbol indicating the length of the pause. See "Note Values and Relationships."

Rhythm: A pattern of musical movement characterized by a series of accented and unaccented notes.

Rhythmic notation: Specifies the exact *rhythms* of a musical passage using the symbols of *standard notation*. *Rhythmic notation* alone does not contain any information about which *notes* to play; therefore, in a number *chart*, you would write the *chords* or notes that you would like played above the desired rhythmic notation.

rit.: See *ritardando*.

Ritardando (*ree-tar-DAHN-doh*): Italian word meaning "get gradually slower." It is typically notated with the abbreviation, *rit.*, followed by dots, indicating the duration of the *ritardando*.

Root: The fundamental *note* of a *chord* or *scale*.

Root position: Refers to a *chord* with its *root note* on the bottom. Opposite of *chord inversions*.

Scale: A progression of *notes* in a specific order. See *major scale* and *minor scale*.

Scale degree: The number of each *note* in a *scale*. In a *major scale* (one *octave*) you would count the scale degrees as follows: 1st–2nd–3rd–4th–5th–6th–7th–8th scale degree (*octave* note same as the first). You will typically see *scale degrees* up to a 13th (6th an octave higher).

Second ending: Bracketed section of a *song* to be played during the end of a repeated part of music. Used in conjunction with *first ending*.

|2. ————————
5̣7

Second inversion chords: See *chord inversions*.

Sharp (♯): Symbol that, when placed the left of any number or *note*, raises its pitch by a *half step*.

Short bar: A *Number System* term for any *measure* that is shorter than that of the established *time signature*. *Short bars* are marked on either side with parentheses, and the number of *beats* is indicated by the number of dots over the measure. (1̈)

6/8 time: *Time signature* with six *beats* per *measure* that uses the *eighth note* to represent one beat. Usually interpreted as two triplet beats: **1**–2–3–**4**–5–6.

Sixteenth note (♪): A *note* half the duration of an *eighth note* and sixteenth the duration of a *whole note*. When subdividing in sixteenth notes, verbalize as, "1–ee–&–uh, 2–ee–&–uh, 3–ee–&–uh, 4–ee–&–uh." See "Note Values and Relationships."

Sixteenth rest (𝄿): Holds the same duration as a *sixteenth note*; the *sixteenth rest* tells you to rest, or not play, for that duration. See "Note Values and Relationships."

SOL (*soul*): *Solfege* syllable representing the 5th *scale degree*. Synonymous with 5 in the *Number System*.

Song: A musical composition containing lyrics usually accompanied by instruments.

Split bar: *Number System* term referring to a *measure* containing two evenly spaced *chord* changes. *Split bars* are notated by underlining both of the chords that will appear within that measure. The split bar has a chord beginning on beat 1 and changes chords on beat 3.

Standard notation: The most common and precise notation method, developed in Western Europe in the 1600s, that uses a *staff* of five lines and four spaces to convey the *notes* to be played. The *rhythms* are charted with a series of note values and *rests*. See "Note Values and Relationships."

Standard rhythmic notation: See *rhythmic notation*.

Staff: Group of five lines and four spaces used in *standard notation*.

Subdivide: To divide the *beats* into smaller parts. Subdividing the *beat* is often the key to maintaining a steady *tempo*. See *eighth note* and *sixteenth note* for their respective vocalizations.

Syncopated: Unexpected *rhythms* that deviate from the normal rhythmic patterns that have been established during the composition. In number *charts*, highly syncopated rhythms can be notated using *standard rhythmic notation*.

Tempo: Speed at which music is to be played measured in *beats* per minute. This *tempo* marking should be written in the top right hand corner of your *chart*.

TI (*tee*): *Solfege* syllable representing the 7th *scale degree*. Synonymous with 7 in the *Number System*.

Tie (⌒): A curved line connecting two *chords* indicating that they should be sustained as one continuous chord.

Time signature: Shorthand used to explain the meter of a *song* that is expressed as a pair of numbers stacked one on top of the other. The top number tells the player *beats* per *measure*, while the bottom number tell the player which type of *note* will represent one *beat*. Example: $\frac{4}{4}$.

Treble clef (𝄞): Symbol used on the musical *staff* denoting the following note-to-staff assignments:

Triad: A *chord* using three *notes*: the *root*, 3rd, and 5th.

Triplet: A grouping of three even *notes* sometimes occurring over the course of one *beat*.

Turn: See *turnaround*.

Turnaround: Musical interlude that connects sections. A typical *turnaround* falls between the *chorus* and second *verse* and uses similar musical motifs as the *intro*.

Uneven Split bars: *Number System* term referring to bars that have more than one *chord*, but the *measure* is not split equally between the two chords. Notation of an *uneven split bar* is achieved using dots above each chord number to determine how many *beats* to play each chord: 1̈   5̇

Verse: Section of a *song* that tells the story and usually precedes the *chorus*.

Whole note (o): A *note* equal to two *half notes* or four *quarter notes*. A *whole note* takes up an entire measure. This is the origin of the *diamond* symbol used in the *Number System*. See "Note Values and Relationships."

Whole rest (▬): Holds the same duration as the *whole note*; the *whole rest* tells you to rest, or not play, for that duration. See section on "Note Values and Relationships."

Whole step: Equal to two *half steps*. *Whole steps* and half steps in combination are used to build *scales*.

Note Values and Relationships

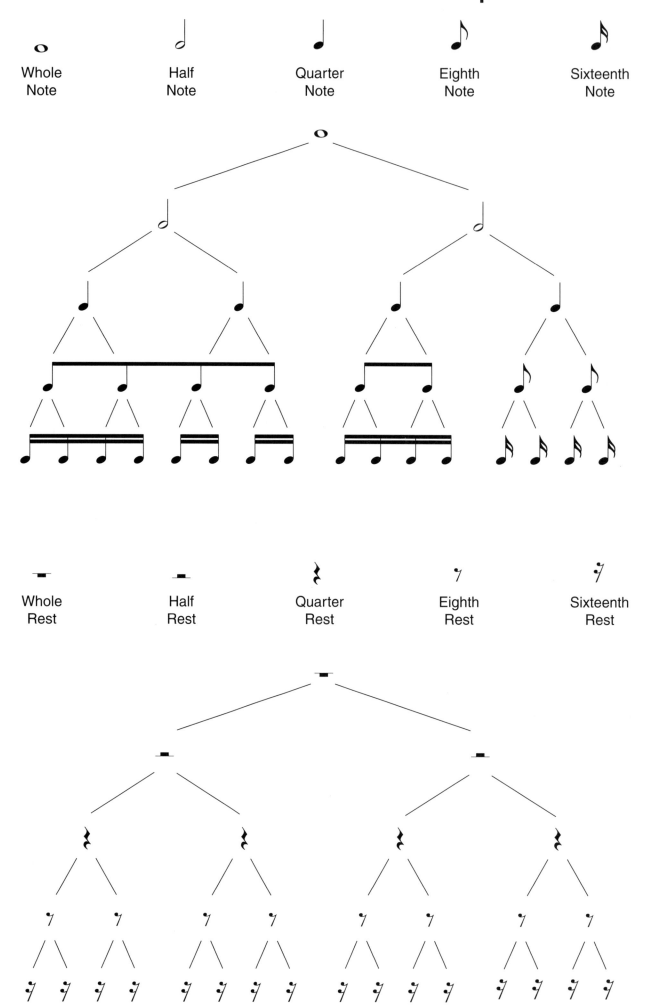

Song Lyrics

Rock and Roll Will Set Me Free

Words and Music by
Jim Riley

Verse

Been on the road my whole career
Havin' to tell my family, "See ya, for a little while."
If my conscience had a voice
And it asked me if I had a choice,
Would I change the road that I've been travelin' on?

Chorus

I've been all around the world just playin' my music
To all the rockin' boys and girls who dig my sound.
And if my conscience ever gets to me,
Rock and roll will set me free.

Verse

Life on the road, it ain't so easy;
Sometimes the food is bad, and the hotel's sleazy.
You're up all night and sleep 'till 1,
But that's when I get my best work done.
Up on the stage is where my heart has always been.

Chorus (2 times)

The Rest of Me

Words and Music by
Jim Riley

Verse

I'm on my best behavior, you're in your Sunday best,
But we both know that we're acting like some other person.
'Cause if we admit to ourselves, there's got to be something more
Than the cars we drive and our pleasant conversation.

Chorus

When you are next to me, you get the best of me.
But when you're gone, I don't know how to feel.
The problem that vexes me is sharing the rest of me.
Showing my imperfections makes this thing too real, if you're wanting the rest of me.

Verse

I'm asking you, babe, to think this through, and make sure it's what you want,
'Cause I'm pretty sure that it won't be all wine and roses.
The one thing that I can promise, I know that it won't be dull
Just as long as you and I are here together.

Chorus

Bridge

You're gonna have to realize, no matter how hard that I try,
There are some things about me that you can never change, you can never change.

Chorus

52

Shooting Stars

Words and Music by
Jim Riley

Verse

Every day I feel like I'm climbing up a hill

On my way to a destiny that I always thought was mine.

Come what may, I have always stood my ground, but I have

Got to say that, "I always thought it'd be easier than this."

Having to prove myself a hundred million times.

But if it's what I've got to do, I'm willing.

Chorus

Even shooting stars have got to find their way in the universe.

All I've ever tried to do is keep this life in drive and never shift into reverse.

Verse

Even the sunshine has got to wake up early to bring us a brighter day.

I know tomorrow I'm gonna have to work twice as hard as I did today.

The only reason that the people I meet think I can't do this is

They don't have what it takes to keep the dream alive.

The one that I dared to dream since I was four or five,

And I ain't stopping now, 'cause I know...

Chorus

Bridge

Even though that I don't know the road ahead,

In my heart, I've always known exactly where it led.

So come with me, take my hand.

Let's find out where you and I will land.

Chorus (2 times)

Right Here

Words and Music by
Jim Riley

Verse

I know that you told me that you didn't want to see me for a while,

But my heart has been aching, and I was just hoping to see your familiar smile.

I know I've got some nerve and I don't deserve one minute more with you.

The truth is: I'm here to surrender, what can I do?

Chorus

How can I make this go away?

How can I take this pain away from you?

All that I want's for you to stay.

I cannot bear to take this break from you.

Please won't you stay just one more day?

All that you need is right here.

Verse

I guess "sorry" won't cut it; I pushed you a little far this time

When I didn't come home and I left you alone, I knew that I crossed the line.

If you'll take me back, we can get on track to the life that we had planned.

I'm just here to make amends; I'm at your command.

Chorus

Bridge

With you by my side, I feel like I can do most anything.

But without you in my life, I don't know what to do.

Won't you please come and save me?

Chorus

Reach Out

MUSIC AND LYRICS BY
JIM RILEY

VERSE

Whenever I look into your brown eyes,

It reminds me of the sandy beach where you and I first met.

You were playing beach ball with your friends,

But when you ran into me, I found a love I wouldn't soon forget.

CHORUS

Now, I'm not saying that it's been all sunny days;

There has been a storm or two.

When I need to get in touch with the things that really matter,

All I have to do is reach out to you.

VERSE

There's not a feeling in this world that's better than the one I have,

Waking up each morning next to you.

We may have traded palm trees for a mini van,

But I can honestly tell you that I much prefer the view.

CHORUS

BRIDGE

Whenever you go away, it feels like a rainy day.

When you're stuck inside with nothing to do,

Heaven knows you've got to roam, but when you finally make it home,

The clouds part, and the sky turns blue.

CHORUS

One More Minute with You

Music and lyrics by
Jim Riley

Verse

All that I want, all that I need,

All that I have in this world is here with you, right here with you.

I want you to stay and spend everyday,

Spend every moment of your life with me. But now I see

That if my love for you is not enough to keep you here with me,

Well, then it's time to pull my heart back 'cause you will never see.

Chorus

What we had was so much more than you deserved.

So I'm glad that I didn't waste one more minute with you.

Verse

Whenever they say to spend every day

As if it's your last, I'd say, "they hit the spot, you had your shot."

But I want to know how you could just throw

All that we had out with the weekly trash. It seems so rash,

But I can throw this in with all the disappointment you have caused,

And I can tell you that it's nothing short of true love that you've lost.

Chorus

Bridge

I know you had your reasons.

But I could never figure out why

You gave up so easy

Without ever really trying to work things out and keep this love alive.

Chorus (2 times)

THE GIFT

WORDS AND MUSIC BY
JIM RILEY

VERSE

I felt like I'd reached the point
Where true love had passed me by.
My heart was full of doubt,
As I looked for reasons why.
But when true love finds you,
It reminds you
There must be something more
Than just worlds colliding.
Now I'm finding hope outside my door.

CHORUS

All that I have in my life,
I owe to the love that we share.
All that I need in this world
Is to know that you'll always be there.
You're my saving grace.
Nothing in this world could take the place
Of the love you've given me.

VERSE

The days before I met you,
There was no hope in sight
Of finding the love I need
As I looked into the night.
But when your light shines on me,
The whole world sees
The person you perceive.
Now my heart's on fire,
And I aspire
To make sure you believe.

CHORUS

BRIDGE

Through my years of loneliness, there's something I've learned:
That love's the only gift you'll get that's got to be earned.
If you don't work at it, it will wither away.
Now I wouldn't assume a gift like this would be delivered twice.
A love like this may come along but once in your life,
So grab hold of it and seize the day.

CHORUS

57

Feeling's Gone

Words and Music by
Jim Riley

Verse

All my life, all I've heard

Is people telling me that what I've been searching for is right outside that door.

So, naturally, when I met you,

I thought I'd found myself an island in the storm, someone to keep me warm.

Wow, did I have you figured wrong.

You and I may not last until the end of this song!

Chorus

Feeling's gone, and I don't know if I feel the same way.

I'm moving on to somebody new and a brighter day.

Verse

You must think that I'm a fool

If you don't think that I see everything you do and who you do it to.

You can sit there and deny

Everything, but I have seen with my own eyes

It's all a pack of lies.

So go ahead and have your fun,

But don't let yourself pretend that you're the only one.

Chorus (2 times)

Bridge

Save me from your sad excuses.

You're out of here, out the door.

Don't want to see you anymore.

I'm tired of feeling bad

While I watch you lose the best you ever had.

Chorus (2 times)

My Life without You

Words and Music by
Jim Riley

Verse

I guess there's nothing more to say.

You say that it's over,

But I know that I won't be over you.

Why does is have to be this way?

Couldn't we give it one more chance?

You know I think that we can make it.

One day we'll both look back at this time

And wish we'd never crossed that line.

Chorus

You know we had a life that most would love
to lead,

But we didn't stay true.

And while I'd give our love another chance,
you say,

"There's no more that we can do."

So, I guess I'll get on with my life without you.

Verse

Just another cloudy day;

I say, "What's the difference?

They all seem pretty gloomy since you've gone."

It doesn't seem that it would pay

To ever leave your heart exposed

Where someone could just break it.

There was a day where love was our guide,

But without that, I'm lost inside.

Chorus

Bridge

Can you come up with a reason

We shouldn't take another season

To try to make things right?

Even though your heart's been broken,

You can take mine as a token.

I won't give up without a fight.

Verse

It's the dawn of a new day.

Life is just beginning,

At least the new one between you and I.

I think I've finally found my way

And I'm never gonna lose it

As long as I have you here by my side.

Before

Music and lyrics by
Jim Riley

Verse

The night is cold.
I'm reaching out for you, but you're not there.
I long to know where exactly have you gone.
Though I've been told
That you are never coming back,
It's clear to see that I need to hear it from you.

Chorus

Before I bury you
In the farthest recess of my heart,
There's one thing I've got to know:
What is this force that keeps us apart?
I guess I may never know.

Verse

I spend my time
Traveling the world in hopes that I will find
Even the smallest sign that tells me you're still here.
Walking the line between life and death, and it's killing me
To follow you. Won't you please just give me a sign?

Chorus

Bridge

I always felt our love would guide us through our darkest days,
But I feel like I'm going blind.
No longer can I see the path. You've traveled in the haze
To a place I'll never find.

Chorus

Recording Credits

All songs recorded at The Grip recording studio in Nashville, TN.

Produced by Jim Riley
Engineered and mixed by Sean Neff

<u>Musicians</u>
Jim Riley: Drums, percussion

Tim Marks: Bass guitar

Trey Hill: Rhythm guitar

Tim Akers: Piano, organ

Dann Huff: Lead guitar on "Shooting Stars," "Right Here," "Reach Out," "The Gift" and "Before"

Jonathan Trebing: Lead guitar on "One More Minute" and rhythm guitar on audio examples

J.D. Simo: Lead guitar on "Rock and Roll Will Set Me Free"

Jonathan Yudkin: Strings on "My Life Without You"

Charlie Judge: Loop programming and synthesizers on "Before"

John Dedrick: Keyboards on audio examples

Female vocals: Jaime Riley

Male vocals: Jim Riley

All songs written by Jim Riley and used by permission of *Melodic Endeavors Publishing* BMI 2010

Audio Track Listing

Track	Title/Description	Track	Title/Description
01	Audio Example A	23	**"Shooting Stars"**
02	Audio Example B	24	"Shooting Stars" (minus guitars)
03	Dictation Example One	25	"Shooting Stars" (minus keys)
04	**"Rock and Roll Will Set Me Free"**	26	"Shooting Stars" (minus bass)
05	"Rock and Roll Will Set Me Free" (minus guitars)	27	"Shooting Stars" (minus drums)
06	"Rock and Roll Will Set Me Free" (minus keys)	28	Audio Example J
07	"Rock and Roll Will Set Me Free" (minus bass)	29	Audio Example K
08	"Rock and Roll Will Set Me Free" (minus drums)	30	Audio Example L
09	Audio Example C	31	Audio Example M
10	Audio Example D	32	Dictation Example Four
11	Audio Example E	33	**"Right Here"**
12	Dictation Example Two	34	"Right Here" (minus guitars)
13	**"The Rest of Me"**	35	"Right Here" (minus keys)
14	"The Rest of Me" (minus guitars)	36	"Right Here" (minus bass)
15	"The Rest of Me" (minus keys)	37	"Right Here" (minus drums)
16	"The Rest of Me" (minus bass)	38	Audio Example N
17	"The Rest of Me" (minus drums)	39	Audio Example O
18	Audio Example F	40	Audio Example P
19	Audio Example G	41	Audio Example Q
20	Audio Example H	42	Audio Example R
21	Audio Example I	43	Dictation Example Five
22	Dictation Example Three	44	**"Reach Out"**
		45	"Reach Out" (minus guitars)
		46	"Reach Out" (minus keys)
		47	"Reach Out" (minus bass)
		48	"Reach Out" (minus drums)

About the Author

Since 1997, **Jim Riley** has been paving his own unique path in Nashville, Tennessee. As a performer, Jim has served as the longtime drummer and bandleader for Rascal Flatts. He has played over a thousand shows in sold-out arenas across North America. His television credits include *The Tonight Show* and the GRAMMYS®. His recording credits include artists such as Rascal Flatts and Brian McKnight. He has also performed with Carrie Underwood, Gary Allan, Vince Gill, Mark Chesnutt and Jessica Simpson, to name a few. Jim was voted Best Country Drummer by the readers of *Drum!* magazine three years in a row. As an educator, Jim is in demand as an international clinician. He was voted Best Drum Clinician by the readers of *Modern Drummer* magazine. In 2007, he opened the doors to his teaching studio, The Drum Dojo, where he teaches percussion classes and private lessons. Jim also keeps busy as a freelance producer creating music for clients all across the U.S.

Jim was born in Boston, Massachusetts and, from an early age, exhibited exceptional musical talent. He began his formal studies as a percussionist at age 12, the same year he began singing with the Youth Pro Musica Choir. In high school, Jim began his studies with Boston Symphony Orchestra percussionist, Arthur Press. In addition to participating in his school's band program, Jim was also performing with the Greater Boston Youth Symphony Orchestra and the Massachusetts Youth Wind Ensemble. He was also elected to All State his final three years of high school.

Upon graduation, he attended the University of North Texas, where he earned a degree in Music Education. During his tenure at UNT, he studied drums with Ed Soph, and timpani with the Dallas Symphony's Kal Cherry. Jim was also heavily involved with their internationally-acclaimed jazz program, as well as performing in the top orchestra, wind ensemble, and percussion ensemble at the university. In the area of marching percussion, Jim performed with the UNT drumline, which won five national championships during his tenure. He also played in the Drum Corps International Finals as a member of the Velvet Knights Drum and Bugle Corps. For more information on Jim, please visit **www.jimrileymusic.com**.

Jim is sponsored by Ludwig, Sabian, Remo, Gibraltar, Vater, and Shure.